Peaches 19 and the Cobras

PAULA BAILEY

To order additional copies of this book, contact:
Xlibris
844-714-8691
www.Xlibris.com
Orders@Xlibris.com

ISBN: 978-1-6641-7061-2 (sc)
ISBN: 978-1-6641-7059-9 (hc)
ISBN: 978-1-6641-7060-5 (e)

Library of Congress Control Number: 2021908282

Print information available on the last page

Rev. date: 05/28/2021

INTRODUCTION

I hope you enjoy our little story about our adventures and our life during the pandemic of 2020. You know, when you're home alone all this time, quarantined with two dogs, you're talking to them all the time, and then you start thinking like them; thus, **19 Cobras** *came to be. Peaches and Jake are two amazing rescue dogs that I've had since they were three years old. Jake is ten now, and Peaches is seven. They keep me entertained, make me laugh a lot, and are my constant companions. In short, they are my babies. So I wanted to share some of their antics with you.*

19 Cobras *is an entertaining book that puts a little humor into a very serious time in our lives. I hope you get a chuckle or two out of it. It was written to help take our minds off the sad things that were happening and put some happy thoughts into our lives, even if it is just for a little while and remind us all how truly blessed we are. Now, sit back, put your feet up, relax, and get ready to smile.*

♥ Always,
Paula Bailey

I KNOW I HEARD WHAT I THOUGHT I HEARD

Hello, my name is Peaches, and this is my big brother, Jake. Jake is my best friend, and he's really smart and *very brave*! We're sitting in our front room at our house in Florida. This is my story about the 19 Cobras and the pandemic here in 2020.

It seems that sometime late in 2019, there was this really *bad* virus that started in China, and it was spreading everywhere—all over the world! Early in 2020, it came to our country, and on March 11, this virus became very serious here, so serious that our government declared it a *pandemic*. Mommy says that means it has spread everywhere! I heard them saying on TV that we should all protect ourselves by staying home, and if we *do* go out, we should wear a mask and wash our paws—I mean, *hands*—a lot and stay away from crowds. I kept hearing them talking about "19 Cobras" on the news. They kept saying, "19 Cobras this" and "19 Cobras that," so I guess that's the name of the new virus, "19 Cobras."

IT'S ALL ABOUT WHAT YOU (THINK) YOU HEAR

What I heard them say on the news was that there were these cobras—19 of them, and if one *got* you, and you got infected, then you could infect other people you got close to, and that is how this virus was spreading, because people would get sick and lots of us would die just by touching something one of those sick people touched or by just breathing their air!

I'M NOT TALL! (BUT I DO HAVE A TAIL)

Now, Mommy says I sometimes like to tell a tall tale, but just look at me—I am *really short.* I have *very* short legs, so just how in the world could I tell a tall tale with these short legs? There's just no way!

Oh man, I was pretty scared when I heard about those 19 Cobras and that they were causing people all over the world to get sick and *die*! And that if one *got* you, or if you *got* it, you were *doomed*!

THE MAN OF THE HOUSE

Since Jake considered himself the "Man of the House", he was worried about protecting me and Mommy from those 19 Cobras.

He was always on the lookout for them. He would walk around in the house checking to make sure everything was safe, and then he would go outside and do the same thing. If we went bye-bye in the car, his eyes were always scanning the streets to make sure we were safe. When we were home, after checking inside the house, he would go out on the front porch to see if any cobras were trying to sneak up the street. Then he would look around the front and backyard and then go check out the dock to make sure that none of them were trying to sneak up the canal we live on to get us! He was *obsessed* with keeping us safe.

INSPECTOR JAKE

I already told you how particular Jake was about constantly checking inside and outside our house to make sure we stayed safe, but that's *nothing* compared to when we received gifts and packages that had been ordered online because Mommy couldn't go out to shop like she used to. Many of the shops and stores were only selling things online, and so people had to either call or order things on their computer, and those things had to be delivered to them. I think it was very confusing at first, but people adapted, and more and more of them seemed to like shopping that way.

Anyway, as I started to tell you, if someone came to our house to repair or fix something—**look out!** You were frisked, and your pockets were gone through before you got very far! Jake was just making sure that none of the awful things had tried to hide in someone's pockets or equipment bags. Jake inspected all packages and boxes delivered to the house, and to complicate things even more, Mommy had a birthday and was getting presents and packages delivered too. So Jake was going through each one to make sure it was okay and safe for Mommy

to open. It fascinated and amazed me how he would just stick his whole head down in a bag or package to check it out. Well, he would *sniff* it first to make sure it didn't smell funny. (I guess cobras have a *"strange smell"*—**I don't know, that's just what Jake told me!**) I tried it, but it was too scary for me! He was *thorough* and *very brave*, and he took his assignment *very* seriously! We definitely felt safe with him on duty.

JAKE CAN BE TRICKY

Jake can be kind of tricky sometimes. Just look at him checking out our pest control technician's pants pockets making us think it's just because one of those 19 Cobras might have hitched a ride in her pocket without her knowing it, and he's just doing his job checking to make sure it's safe for her to come into the rest of the house. But *really,* he knows that she keeps doggie treats in that pocket, and he's just helping himself to a few! She always gives me some, and all I have to do is sit here and look cute, so I'm not worried that I won't get any.

BEING QUARANTINED

So we needed to be *very* careful and stay inside and wash our paws—I mean, *hands*—all the time. They called it being quarantined.

JUST FOOL'N

Jake just cracks me up sometimes! He thought if we were quarantined, that meant we needed to go inside and get under something—he got under Mommy's table!

So when I told him that wasn't what they meant about being quarantined, Jake said, "Heh-heh-heh, I knew that! I was just fool'n you!" (You can't tell it here, but I'm rolling my eyes right now because I think—*he* thinks—I bought that story! Oh well, I'll just let him believe that!)

JAKE'S CRAZY OUTFIT

Jake was so funny he even put on this crazy outfit and tried to put on his *mean face* to try to take Mommy's and my minds off the 19 Cobras. He said he was going to go out and scare those cobras with this outfit, but *we* knew he was just trying to keep our minds off of the danger by clowning around!

THE SHELVES ARE ALMOST EMPTY!

I guess people started to panic because I heard grocery stores were running out of food and supplies. They even ran out of toilet paper and paper towels, for heaven's sake! Their shelves were empty of almost everything! (I'm sure glad Jake and I don't have to use toilet paper—that could be a serious problem!)

JAKE'S ADVICE

Then Jake said to me, "You know, Peaches, we don't know how long these 19 Cobras are going to be around, and this is pretty serious stuff. Mommy might get a little stressed, so we need to be as good as we can and try to keep her busy so she doesn't have to worry too much, especially about us."

MOMMY GETS US PREPARED

Mommy put these patriotic bandanas on us just in case we needed to go out into a crowd of people we'd be protected. Mine looks pretty long; I hope I don't step on it and trip or fall—that would be embarrassing!

JAKE IS THE BEST BIG BROTHER EVER!

Jake showed me how I'm supposed to put the bandana over my nose and mouth. (I hope I don't have to keep it there too long!) Jake is so smart, and such a good big brother. He always watches out for me and knows just what to do!

MATCHING MASKS

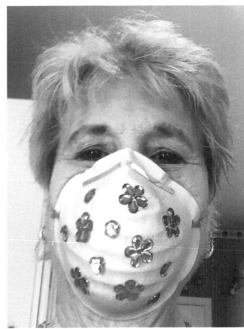

They are telling everyone on the news that if we go outside and are anywhere around people, we need to wear a mask. So Mommy decides it would be fun to make matching masks for us. (I think she just needs something to do to keep her mind off of the 19 Cobras.) The masks are really pretty! They have jewels and sparkles and everything! Mommy puts hers on to show us how to wear them, and Jake and I look at each other and I say, *"Oh no, you don't! Huh-uh, no way! That covers our nose and mouth, and it will smother us!"* But Mommy has other ideas. She wants a picture, and she has her mind made up. And what Mommy wants, she (usually) gets—eventually, anyway!

THE WARNING!

I whispered in Jake's ear to get prepared. Mommy had a big plan to try to get those new masks on us to take a picture, and we might get *smothered*! So we should try to act calm and nonchalant. But Jake doesn't *act* very well (or maybe he just doesn't know what *nonchalant* means) because he gets this panicked and mortified look on his face—*see*!

THE TALE OF THE DIFFICULT MASKS

So round and round we went, Mommy trying to get the masks to stay on us long enough to get a picture, and Jake and I determined we were destined to *die* if the mask covered our nose and mouth. Mommy would put a mask on each of us, turn around to get the camera, and by the time she turned back around, we had our masks off and were sitting there smiling and looking innocent.

IT'S LIKE A THREE-RING CIRCUS!

Mommy described it later as pretty much like a three-ring circus! Whenever she had her back turned, Jake and I were getting our masks off and planning our next move. We **were** being pretty mischievous!

PLAYING TRICKS ON MOMMY

One time, we ditched the masks and changed our bandanas so she wouldn't recognize us then ran and hid in the living room, but she found us. (I think we were snickering and chuckling too loud.) We couldn't help it! It was just so funny, and we were having so much fun playing tricks on Mommy!

THE FINAL STRAW

It got to be pretty comical, but I think the final straw was when we had the masks on top of our heads! That's when Mommy gave us "THE LOOK," and Jake said, "Uh-oh, I think she means business now! We'd better shape up and do what she wants us to do, or we might get *spanked*!" (I still don't know what "spanked" is, but I don't think it's good.)

IT WAS A DISASTER!

So we let Mommy put our masks on us to get the picture, but my mask was too **big** and kept going over my eyes, **and I couldn't SEE**! And Jake said his mask was too **"girly"** with the jewels and sparkles and that he was a **Big Boy**, and anyway, his strap broke so his wouldn't stay on.

WE GOT NEW MASKS!

So Mommy made us some new masks, and we are very happy now. Jake likes his because it doesn't have any sparkles or jewels and is more *manly*. And I **LOVE** mine because *I can see*, and *it sparkles* **AND** *it matches my bows*! But the **very best** thing is, <u>we aren't smothering after all!</u>

HAPPY BIRTHDAY TO ME!

Today is my seventh birthday, and Mommy made me these new bows for my birthday. I love them because they are bright and shiny, and Mommy says they sparkle—*just like my eyes*!

And Mommy made some very special doggie cupcakes with special icing just for me! Then Mommy and Alexa—you know who Alexa is, don't you? Alexa is like a member of our family! She is in every room of our house, and she is **very** smart! She can tell you the news, the weather,

how to spell a word, she plays music, sings songs, and even tells jokes! She knows almost everything—well, almost. Anyway, as I was saying, Mommy and Alexa sang "Happy Birthday" (and I had to sit still and act like they could carry a tune—especially Mommy—oh boy!) But after they sang, Jake and I got to eat *two* cupcakes each, and we got ice cream! And that was really yummy and special!

OUR MAGICAL FAIRYLAND

Mommy really makes our house look pretty at Christmastime. When she takes us out for a walk after dark, this is what our house looks like from the outside with the Christmas trees lit. But it looks the prettiest from the back because there are more windows on the back of the house, and Jake and I get to see this when we go out in the backyard to potty. I told Jake it looks like a *Magical Fairyland!*

SOME OF MOMMY'S FOURTEEN CHRISTMAS TREES

Vero Beach Garden Club

It's a Wonderful Life

Secret   Patriotic
Service

Master Bedroom Trees

"Angel"

9-1-1   "Angel"   "Ellie"

"Ellie" (Elegant)

Mama's Tree

Travel

9-1-1

THE REST OF MOMMY'S FOURTEEN CHRISTMAS TREES

Statue of Liberty

Apple

By the Sea

Mommy loves Christmastime, and she loves to decorate for Christmas. This year, she had fourteen Christmas trees that she decorated for our house. We even had a Christmas tree in our *bathtub* because Mommy said she ran out of places to put them! They were all themed and were decorated with ornaments that she has been given by friends or ones she has collected over the years. She says each ornament has a special meaning or memory that goes along with it, and they bring back such wonderful memories and make her very happy. So when the 19 Cobras pandemic came, she left her trees up to help cheer all of us up. She said her neighbors probably thought she was nuts, but Jake and I thought it was a *great* idea because it made our house look cheerful and made us happy too!

White House Miniatures

White House Historical Society

I WONDER ...

Sometimes I wonder if our Christmas trees scare the 19 Cobras. I think about all the trees we have and how pretty they are all lit up at nighttime looking at our house from the outside (and the inside too) and think that maybe the cobras think this is a safe place or safety zone for anyone but them, and all the bright shining lights make it look like a *magical place* they can't be, or *they* will die! That's not why Mommy left all our trees up. She was expecting overnight guests in March, and she wanted them to see her trees so that's why she left them up. But when the 19 Cobras came, she decided that we all needed the cheerful atmosphere the trees brought to our home, so she left them up to keep our spirits up. And they do! Just look at these pretty trees; each one is different, and each one is bright and shiny, and I just can't keep that smile off my face when I look at them. They make me so happy I could do backflips around the house, but I don't want to right now. It's not that I don't know *how* to do a backflip. I just don't *want* to do any right now, **OK?**

LET'S REDO THE BATHROOM!

When we were quarantined and were supposed to stay home, Mommy was about to climb the walls, so she decided to reorganize and redecorate her bathroom. Boy, what a job that was! In fact, nobody—not me, not Jake, not even our housekeeper, Sandra— was allowed in there while Mommy was cleaning out those closets, cupboards, and drawers! (It was a good thing. Holy cow, just look at that mess!) Uh-oh, don't tell Mommy I said that or that I sneaked in and took these pictures. I don't want to hurt her feelings (or get in trouble). She worked so hard!

WHAT A DIFFERENCE!

But this is the end result. Doesn't it look nice! Mommy said only one more thing needed to be changed to make everything look coordinated. The Statue of Liberty Christmas tree (in the bathtub) needed to be changed to the new theme, which was .. *shells*! So ..

Meet Shelly!

Isn't she beautiful?

SANDRA

This is Sandra; she is Mommy's housekeeper, but Mommy says she is so much more than that. She is Mommy's friend, helper, and right hand. I didn't know Mommy had two right hands, maybe that's like having eyes in the back of your head, because Mommy *does* sometimes. I *know* she does because how else would she be able to tell that I'm picking on Jake? He won't tell, or he'd be on *my* list, and he really doesn't want to be on my list because I might be little, but I'm *mighty!* Mommy says Sandra is *her* boss instead of the other way around, because Sandra *always* knows just what to do! She says they make a great team. In addition, Sandra is our babysitter, friend, and substitute Mommy when Mommy has to go away and can't take us with her. It was Sandra who came up with the idea to put that "lid thing" on the tub for the Christmas tree, and whenever she mentions an idea to Mommy, they get their heads together, then ***look out***! Amazing things happen!

BYE-BYE BATHTUB

I guess that "lid thing" is called a platform because I heard Mommy and Sandra asking Uncle Dick and Aunt Katt if they would help make a platform to cover the bathtub so that our new tree could sit inside. Mommy said Uncle Dick was the perfect person to do the job because he was so particular, and she knew the job would be done to perfection if he did it. He even made a little stool for the tree stand to sit on inside the tub so it would be very sturdy and straight. After the platform was made, Mommy brought it home from Uncle Dick's house and Sandra tweaked it. Mommy said, "It fits like a glove" (whatever that means, because it sure doesn't look like a glove).

HELLO, SHELLY

They added some carpet to make it look like sand and lined the outside of the platform with tiny little shells to make it look pretty. Then, Mommy put some *very big* special shells under the tree that she had collected in the Bahamas a long time ago with her sweetie. (That's the name she called her husband who died, but not from 19 Cobras. This was a *long* time ago, Mommy said.) So our new tree in the bathtub was all decorated with shells, and of course, we named it Shelly, but you already knew that, didn't you?

BEING A HOSTAGE IN YOUR OWN HOME!

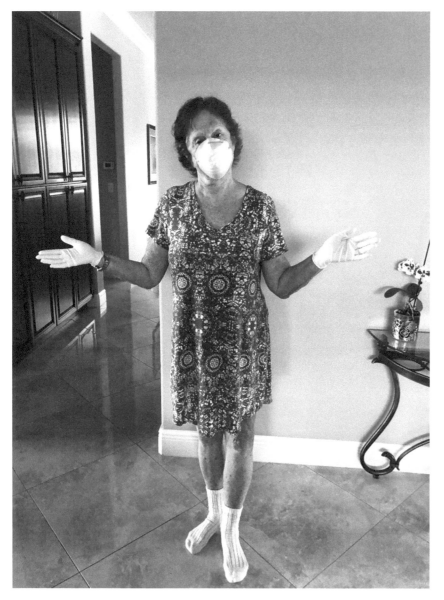

This is Carole, Mommy's best friend in Florida. She and her husband can't go out because they are very compromised due to their health, so they need to have things delivered to them at their home. This is the outfit she wears when she answers the door—isn't she cute? She says she looks terrible in this picture because she doesn't have her eyebrows on. I think she looks pretty just the way she is. What are eyebrows?

SOCIAL DISTANCING

They tell us to practice social distancing. This is Aunt Deb and Uncle Rich with their neighbors in their driveway at their new house in northern Florida, practicing social distancing. They are celebrating Uncle Rich's first ProgRock Podcast. Mommy says ProgRock is a type of music and a podcast is like a radio show. Everyone brought their own drinks and chairs and were at least six feet apart because Aunt Deb says, **"That's the rules!"**

MOMMY KEEPS OUT OF TROUBLE

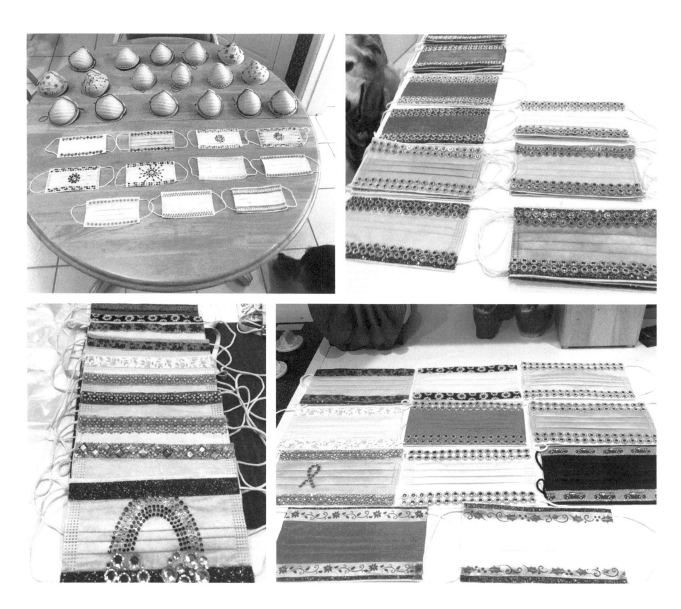

Now, I want to tell you a little bit more about what we did while we were quarantined to pass the time. Of course, Jake was pretty busy making sure we were safe from the 19 Cobras. I kind of helped him when I could and also stayed pretty close to Mommy in case she needed me. Mommy always found things to do to keep from getting bored. She started decorating these paper masks for fun and to just keep busy, and then she would give them away to friends and family. They were thrilled! She said it "kept her out of trouble." (I thought Jake and I were the only ones who got into trouble around here!)

LOOKING GOOD!

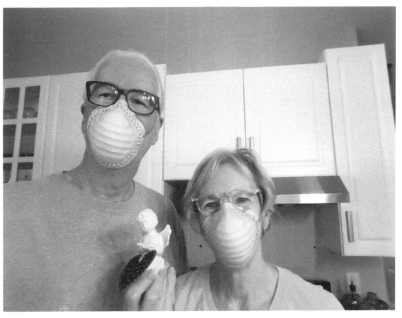

Here are some of Mommy's relatives wearing the masks she made for them. (Not the dog, silly, that's Phoebe. She belongs to Kyle and Ashley.) They all sent Mommy these pictures of them in their masks to show her how good they looked!

MOMMY GIVES BACK

Mommy also makes these "Special Angels" that she gives to the first responders, caregivers, those people whom she feels have made a difference in her life over the years—her family and friends, people who work for her, delivery people, doctors and their staff, and other deserving people she meets.

ANGELS AMONG US

Here are some of Mommy's angels (and masks) in their new homes.

WE MISS YOU!

Mommy helped Jake and me send some flowers to *our* favorite friends to let them know that we missed them. Aren't these flowers that we picked out pretty!

COMMUNITY SUPPORT

Now when I get to go bye-bye with Mommy in the car, we see several signs like these thanking and supporting our first responders and caregivers. *Yay!*

TRAVELING IN THE RV

Jake and I love traveling in the RV. We have a lot of room to move around inside, and Mommy had a special seat made for us that goes across the passenger seat and console so we both can sit up front with her and look out the front and side windows or stretch out and take a nap if we want to. It works out great, and there's no need for us to move around until we stop because we have everything we need right there. So when we travel to and from Maine each year, we are very comfortable.

When we get to a campground, we usually stay for a couple of nights, and we have a lot of fun exploring the new things there, and there are *always* a lot of new **smells** for us to try to figure out! We *love* being outside, and this is just the ultimate!

MAINE

I want to tell you some things about our life in Maine because we love it up there so much and we really miss our friends and the things we do up there. It is completely different than life in Florida, but in a good way, and we will still have to look out for the 19 Cobras because they are *everywhere*!

This is Mommy's cottage in Maine where we spend our summers. It makes me homesick when I look at these pictures because we have made a lot of friends there, and we really love to spend our summers there. But *not* wintertime. Mommy says it gets too cold for her up there, but probably not for Jake and me because we have our *winter coats* on. But if Mommy isn't going to be there, then Jake and I don't want to be there either. *No way!*

COMFY COZY

This is Mommy's bedroom at the cottage; it's really cozy. I get to sleep in Mommy's bed because I can jump *really* high! But Jake has to sleep on the floor now because he can't jump that high anymore. He says that's okay, because he can be on guard better if he's on the floor. I like to take naps on Mommy's bed, and if Mommy's bed is made with all the pillows at the top, I like to make a *nest* right in the middle of them to take my nap. Now that's what I call *pure heaven*!

MOMMY DOESN'T HAVE A GREEN THUMB, REALLY!

Just look at our beautiful flowers that come up every year around our cottage! They are so pretty, and everybody likes them. Mommy says she doesn't have a green thumb—she really doesn't! I checked! So she hired this really nice guy named Brandon to come and take care of her flowers for her. Sometimes his wife, Nannette, comes with him to help. Brandon loves Jake and me, and so does Nannette. We always look forward to them coming to take care of our flowers because we always go outside to greet them, and they give us lots of butt scratches and neck rubs.

GOOD BEHAVIOR

Several of Mommy's friends either have big, gigantic motor homes or cottages near ours in Maine, but no pets, so they can pay extra special attention to Jake and me. Mommy always warns us that we had better be on our *best* behavior because they aren't used to having *four-legged youngsters* like us around. But it's not hard to be good around them because we really, really like all of them (and I think they really like us because I am so *adorable* and Jake is so *smart!*)

Tom and Nancy
(Cottage)

Nelda and Gerald
(BIG Motorhome)

Barb and Dick
(Cottage)

Carole and George
(BIG Motorhome)

"Cutie Pie"

"Smartie Pants"

WE GET READY FOR A LUAU

Our friends from Florida, Paula and Jim, are getting Jake and me ready for a Luau. I don't really know what that is, but I think it's some kind of Hawaiian party or celebration because we all get to wear these pretty flower necklaces—*me and Jake too*! And then Mommy's friend, Paula, made some special kind of drink called a mai tai. It had some yummy looking fruit in it. Mommy said it was some pineapple and a cherry! (I don't know, but it looked like I might like to eat that cherry!)

Don't I look cute in my flower necklace? Mommy says it's called a lei; it sounds like "lay," but Mommy says it's spelled differently because it's Hawaiian. Anyway, by its name, you'd think it would make you lay down. Huh, well, I guess maybe there might be some truth to that!

WHEN KIDS COME TO VISIT

We especially like it when kids come to visit. Some stay at other cottages. Usually, they ask Mommy if we can come out and play with them in the central play area. The people who live behind us had their four grandchildren—Makayla, Micah, Elijah, and Kaleb—visiting them for a couple of weeks, and we got to play together every day! We had so much fun, and we got lots of exercise and lots of great doggie pats and attention! Jake and I didn't want them to leave.

HOW WE START OUR DAY ... EXCEPT SOMETIMES (WHEN WE DON'T)

We like to sleep a little later in the morning in Maine because it's pretty cool early in the morning, and Mommy and I like to snuggle under the covers to keep warm a little longer. But we get up about nine. Well, I should say Mommy gets up about nine. I get to stay in bed until she gets ready to go outside to take us for our morning walk. That's because I don't have to take a shower, get dressed, put on any makeup, do my hair, and all the other things humans do when they get up. It's exhausting!

But Mommy always looks very nice when we go for our morning walk. We walk around the cottages, and our friend, Louella, comes out from her cottage to say hi, and she always has a tasty treat for Jake and me. At first, I think Louella was a little bit afraid of dogs, but we quickly changed her mind and showed her how kind and loving we can be (in addition to being beyond cute)! Louella and Mommy have become very close friends, and we always look forward to seeing her every day.

Jake and I look at Louella's cottage to see if she's there because she hasn't come to see us today. Jake checks out their other cottage, but she's not there either, but we'll see her later because Mommy and The Girl's Lunch Bunch, (that's what they call themselves), are getting together later for lunch as they do every Friday. Mommy has a picture book she made starring me and Jake that she wants to show them.

This is Mommy showing her lunch friends, Ann and Louella, her picture books. The *very best* one is the one that stars Jake and me!

WHEN OUR FAMILY COMES TO MAINE, WE EAT LOBSTER!

We show Lauren and Phoebe where they are going to have their lobster dinner. Then Mommy, Aunt Deb, and Lauren enjoy their *lobster feast* in our front yard!

And then some more of Mommy's relatives come to visit, and they have their lobster dinner on Mommy's front porch.

LET'S RENAME THIS VIRUS!

Mommy drinks wine, but a lot of her friends drink beer—Corona Beer—and they said, "*Coronavirus,* huh, how can something that bad be the same name of something that tastes so good?" So Mommy said, "Well, let's just rename the virus the *crapola virus* then!" So that's what they started calling it!

"COVID" VS "COBRA"

But they have tests you can take now, and these tests will let you know if you have COVID-19. Oh really? What do *you* think, Jake?

Mommy said this bad virus is *not* about cobra snakes (like I thought), that its name is co-*vid* 19 (not co-*bra* like the snake and like I thought it was called)— whew. And she said that COVID-19 was the name of the *coronavirus* for this year that started in China and was spreading everywhere.

Well, there's one way to find out. Come on, Peaches, let's go check it out!

THE RAPID TEST KIT—NOT

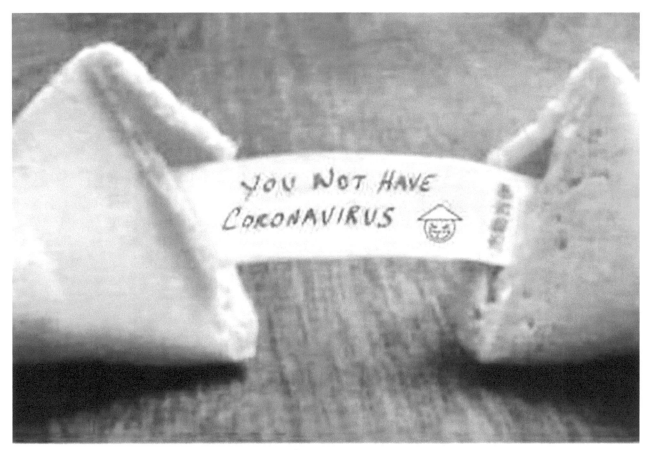

Just received my COVID-19 rapid test kit from CHINA! soooooo relieved!!!!!! Thanks beijing!!!!

Well, would you just look at that, Peaches? A rapid test kit from China! And it seems like it's pretty easy to take with immediate results (and it looks like you get to *eat* the cookie/container it comes in!) *Cool!* The note says, "Just received my COVID-19 rapid test kit from China!" Sooooo relieved! Thanks, Beijing!

PEACHES FIGHTS BACK

Oh, Jake, you're *always* thinking about food and your stomach! I'm not so sure about *that* particular rapid test kit. I think somebody is playing a joke, but Mommy says they *do* have other tests that are more reliable. Well, here's my response to all this nonsense here: "Take that, you 19 Cobras! Or COVID-19!" (Whatever!) Right, Jake?

Now I'm going to go out on our porch and try to give them a really scary look and my Warrior Battle Yell (that I just made up) too! Now, you know I've never done this, Jake, so I'm not sure how this is going to turn out, but I've got to try scaring them in addition to just giving them the *"raspberries"*, so they know I mean business and that they can't play with our emotions like that!

I've got to get my stance just right and concentrate real hard to get myself ready for this! I'm squinting my eyes and everything to look as mean as I can!

Oh, I am so ready now! Here goes!

HI-YA! TAKE THAT, YOU *"JOKESTERS"*!

PEACHES SAFETY RULES

Well, there you go, that's about it. Bye for now, and everybody, please remember: **Wear a mask, wash your hands, practice social distancing, and *most of all,* STAY SAFE! (Because Peaches said so!)**

BYE FOR NOW

We hope you enjoyed our story; it's true, you know. This is how we lived our lives with our Mommy during the 2020 COVID-19 pandemic—from March to December anyway. We enjoyed sharing our lives, friends, and some pre-pandemic memories and experiences with you and hope you liked hearing about them too. We like to be happy and positive about things, and we love to laugh and have fun and try to help others around us enjoy life too.

To be continued ..

Lightning Source UK Ltd.
Milton Keynes UK
UKHW051920060621
384968UK00002B/23